HAVING BEEN A SOLDIER

ERNEST HOLMES

Copyright © 2022 by Ernest Holmes.

All rights reserved. No part of this publication may be reproduced, distributed, or transmitted in any form or by any means, including photocopying, recording, or other electronic or mechanical methods, without the prior written permission of the author, except in the case of brief quotations embodied in critical reviews and certain other noncommercial uses permitted by copyright law.

Printed in the United States of America.

Library of Congress Control Number: 2022934319

ISBN	Paperback	978-1-68536-406-9
	eBook	978-1-68536-407-6

Westwood Books Publishing LLC
Atlanta Financial Center
3343 Peachtree Rd NE Ste 145-725
Atlanta, GA 30326

www.westwoodbookspublishing.com

BOOK 1

CONTENTS

Chapter 1: Beginnings and Catterick. 1

Chapter 2: Tidworth and Squashed Toes. 18

Chapter 3: Hong Kong KamTin and other Incidents. 34

Chapter 4: Libya Sand and Dust .53

Chapter 5: Cyprus and the UN 64

Chapter 6: BOVVIE Camp. 68

Chapter 7: Return to Libya & Fire 72

CHAPTER 1

BEGINNINGS AND CATTERICK

I have to admit, lining up with other scrawny teenagers against the back wall of a North Shields fish quay at midnight for a night's work in the hold of a trawler wasn't a particularly smart move in my career to date.

Aged sixteen and an indentured apprentice plater at the Wallsend Slipway on Tyneside I was going nowhere. I couldn't see myself going through those same gate's day in and day out for the rest of my life, I wanted out. Anyway, the lure of five pounds for six hours work throughout the night, knee deep in shoveling fish and ice seemed a damned sight better than £2 pounds ten shillings working at the Slipway for a week. And so, it proved. I came away from that that night wanting to join the first fishing boat that would have me. Unfortunately, this meant that I would be in hock for the next year or so to the company; the first requirement was that I had to pay £200 towards my clothing and wet weather gear. In other words, I would be working in horrendous and dangerous conditions for nothing for the best part of a year. Trawlers in the sixties was a highly paid, millionaire's wages, but it was a suicide mission… think of that when you next eat fish and chips! Time to think of something else.

A few years earlier, a school pal and I had presented ourselves at the Navy Recruitment Office in Newcastle. I had an older cousin Raymond serving in destroyers trying to avoid Icelandic gun boats who were determined to enforce a 200-mile exclusion zone and demanding we leave the cod and haddock to their trawlers.

'The Cod War' of the sixties. Bloody silly really because a decade or so later we handed over all of our fishing rights, courtesy of that treacherous bastard Edward Heath PM, to the Common Market, so as to bribe our way into the EEC. That did us a lot of good didn't it? At the age of 14, I had been rejected as I was too small for the navy, under 5 ft., four feet eleven inches begod! And my dad wouldn't sign the papers either, so that was my naval career shot to blazes. So, following the careers advice at the local Labour Exchange when I left school at fifteen, I took up an apprenticeship.

Some advice I'd been given. "You have two choices, quoth my careers officer at the Labour Exchange sign on in the pits or sign on in the shipyards, which is it to be?" Most if not all of my family were miners or more accurately, dying miners. Lungs. My granddad survived WW1 in the trenches, shot at, shelled, gassed; he was awarded a Military Medal with 11th Battalion the Durham Light Infantry.

Returning to mining and The Rising Sun Colliery Wallsend on Tyne, 'miners' lung' got him in the end. Not before he had had his nightly bath in a warm deep tin tub in front of the range. We, the youngsters on the other hand had our nightly scrub with carbolic soap in a large white sink in the kitchen, cold tap of course, there not being any other. Later a visit to the outside 'netty' or cludgy., the toilet!

There was Uncle Billy who was a lazy bastard and a ne'r do well who had been deported from Canada as a 'Hobo' in the thirties. My hero actually as he had at least shown some enterprise. Uncle Ernie was equally useless never having had a job since he left the navy after National Service, still I liked him. Aside from the constant reminders that it was a career that too would bring about an early demise. The rest were on their last lung or less! Bugger that I thought, apart from that, at my size the sods would have chosen me as a pit pony; I'd have been hauling coal to the knacker's yard and beyond. Shipyards it was, as an apprentice plater. I stuck it for as long as I could but I hated it.

The Wallsend Slipway was dominated by a 200-ton lift crane alongside the Tyne and the yard had a boiler works, which I was attached to as an apprentice plater. I stuck this for the best part of two years and one of the things I recall was before cutting steel plate was pinging a chalk line across the steel plate to get a straight line before burning the steel. I was given mundane tasks as following around one of the platers and grinding down various bits on a grindstone as required. I do remember on one occasion a test weld with a new-fangled welding torch which could weld aluminum, new technology no less in an antiquated and soon to be a redundant industry. The truth was, I was a dead loss as an apprentice plater.

Wallsend Slipway on Tyneside in the sixties. Big 'Geordie' the 200-ton lift crane in the foreground. The boiler shop, in the centre just beyond the crane, was where I worked as an apprentice. Dry dock is empty; The Slipway was the repair yard as part of Swan Hunter the famous ship-builders of Tyneside.

Most of my friends at that time had the sense to head for the engineering workshops and they had skills which lasted them a lifetime. Amongst the monotony, there were some highlights I recall, such as seeing my first 'dead.' Fished out at the quayside, looking pickled grey. Ironically it was also the first time I'd seen a black man, a rarity on Tyneside in the early sixties, and so for years afterwards I was still trying to differentiate between which features were caused genetics and which were the result of an extended bath in the Tyne. On another occasion there was an accident when a scaffold gave way and two blokes were dropped ten feet, one landed on his head and there was blood everywhere! Yuck! My tradesman reacted as quick as a medic in the army, perhaps it was his earlier service as a conscript, I thought at the time, anyway he was on the scene, staunching blood and calling for a medic whilst the rest of the workers were still gaping at the carnage.

Soon after that accident flat caps were done away with and plastic helmets were issued; different colours for different job descriptions. My red and black snazzy flat cap was consigned to the bin. I remember apprentices wore yellow but the one that got everyone's attention, particularly at the Friday afternoon poker school after pay day, was the sight of a white helmet…. a foreman about to hove into view. Duck! The game was always three card brag. As an apprentice I didn't have much to gamble, but what the hell! On one occasion I had three Jacks and scooped the lot! Excellent. My mum was pleased anyway as she sorted my wages, less my living allowance of course. Best bit at the yards by far was meeting Derek a willing mentor if ever I needed one. It was he who got me into wandering and the YHA. The Youth Hostel Association.

At every opportunity I was away with a Bergen on my back. It held my cotton tent, (with no fly-sheet) and festooned with badges.

I hitch-hiked the length and the breadth of the country. Mostly on my own but occasionally with 'Spud' or 'Sab' as companions and this led to my meeting an old India hand 'Nunk' who took me in one wet and windy night and saved me from hypothermia by ordering me, shivering with cold, naked into a warm bath. I suspect today's generation would query his generosity and not rest until he was publicly outed as a homosexual. But not then. What people forget is the trauma of both wars that he and others fought in. Bachelors and spinsters after these events were just folk who lived singly quite happily and not forgetting what they had experienced nor those whom they had lost. Nunk or as he should be remembered, Hawkshaw Powell, an Irish gentleman who was a confirmed bachelor after WW1 who dedicated his services to his fellow men in the services in India through TOC H and The Salvation Army during WW2. When I met him, he was all for the YHA. Notwithstanding my near-death experience from exposure, my mates, Sab and Spud took me down to the local and after quaffing three pints of 'Scrumpy' had to lead me, falling over grass blades and spewing up every five yards or so back to Nunk's place. As far as Nunk was concerned, if you could play Gin Rummy you were very welcome. Once we picked up and invited two soaking wet hitch-hiking trainee lady teachers back to Nunk's, and I was tasked with quickly teaching them the rudiments of gin rummy before they were allowed through the door! Nunk was never happy in female company but that was him, a product of his time. We didn't ask and he would never have told.

Eventually this all led me at seventeen and a half to apply to join the Army. Whilst waiting on my application I went on a youth hosteling and camping tour of Scotland in the summer of 1963, finally hitch hiking up to the far north.

Crossing Annoch Moor in the early hours and soaked to the skin I had another lucky escape; once again on the point of exposure, I turned back to Loch Lomond and the hostel, thankfully someone stopped and gave me a lift. Thank you. I never knew who you were, but whoever you were, you saved my life.

A hot August as I remember and apart from nearly being drowned in my tent in Glen Nevis during a storm, and groping through the fog on top of Ben Nevis, it was a wonderful two weeks on my own and going where I wanted to, or as the hitches dictated. Anyway, I arrived at John of Groats safe and sound and still a virgin, even though I had met many young girls at various hostels.

Viewing the dripping wet landscape of tussocks and a few derelict buildings and a flock of miserable and desolate sheep. ….Err mm, why does anyone want to go there? Fucked if I know! It's a place I suppose and as the current fashion is to ' visit all of the places on your bucket list' that you have always wanted to visit, this could have been one of them. Nah! I expect I did this long before anyone created 'bucket lists.' As for me and to be honest once I got there, I simply shrugged my Bergen onto my shoulders and turned around and headed south. It's the arse end of the world as I know of it, no better than Lands' End which I knew of a from a similar hitch-hiking experience and that was yet another wet and dead-beat dead-end. A bit like Barrow in Furness I suppose; another cul de sac but least that one has the working-class culture of pubs and clubs. Police sirens, drugs and the brawls to liven the place up at night. All I could hear were the desperate bleat of the sheep as they sought to get away from the drunken and whisky crazed locals. I beat a hasty retreat from the Ben Doon Glen.

Time for an Englishman Scotsman Joke.

There was this English chap who wanted to get away for a break, somewhere remote, such as the highlands. Renting a wee cottage, he was enjoying his stay, walking in the hills, doing a bit of fishing and generally unwinding as he relaxed away from the run of the mill city life. One evening he was sitting reading a book by his peat burning fire, warmed up with a wee nip of 'the creature'. When hist there came a knock at the door. He opened it and fell back in astonishment, for standing there was the biggest, hairiest Jock Highlander you have ever seen. The bugger was as Rob Roy McGregor as you could get. From feathered Tam 'o Shanter, ginger bearded face, flax shirt, leather sporran, kilt and a bloody great claymore at his side to the tartan socks in his buckled shoes. All six foot six of him. "McTavish frae the hoose up the glen," he introduced himself, "Saturday nicht our hoose is ha'ing a party, would ye like to come?"

"A party?" quoth our Englishman, "That's very decent of you to invite me to a party Saturday night, certainly, I do love a party, yes I'll be there."

"Aye weel," says McTavish as he turns away, "we'll a' be drinking the whisky ye ken, the creature!" "Fine, I like whisky," says our Englishman. "Aye weel," says McTavish as he turns away once more, "an we'll a' be fechting after the whisky ye ken!" "Fechting?" says our hero, "Oh you mean fighting. Couldn't be better, I do like a drunken scrap, all good fun."

"Aye weel," says McTavish as he turns away again, "an there'll be the sex after the fechting."

"Couldn't be better, what a party, booze, a fight and the promise of sex...can't wait. Err mm just a thought as it's very remote here, who else is coming to your party Mr. McTavish?"

Fixing the English lad with his gimlet eye, McTavish replied, "Jist you and me laddie..........jist you and me!"

And if that's not true, then it should be. It certainly felt believable enough to keep me on my toes for those two weeks.

Still on my return with 10 shillings left over from the £9 I had started out with a fortnight earlier I went off to join the Army, signing on at Newcastle Recruiting Office. This time I did not need my dad's approval as I had signified, I wanted to join his old regiment the Dragoon Guards, he had no objections. My indentured apprenticeship with Wallsend Slipway was annulled as I had opted to serve Queen and Country instead and that trumped any obligation to the company. Bye the bye Wallsend Slipway! (Which like Swan Hunters and the rest of the ship building industry on Tyneside disappeared in the next few years anyway.)

I was posted to Catterick for fucks sake, North Yorkshire. The RAC training depot. If John of Groats and Lands' End were the arse-end of the world then Catterick had to be the arm-pits, halfway up the country. I had been here before but only as an Army brat. It was different then, a place where we could wander unsupervised all day long. Also, the first place that at school I was caned. Probably only six years old. There were some teacher sadists around at that time. I was caned many times after that, caned, slippered and tawsed, the tawse a thick leather belt favoured by Scotch sadists was added to by the whack around the face with a glove…. Head master of Kirkcudbright Academy. Smith, Wilson, I can't remember but whomever, he was a nasty little shit. Who today would slap a child with a glove for throwing snowballs in the playground? The worst slippering occurred at my boarding school in

Germany. Six of the best on the backside for playing up at school was followed up by another six delivered by Mr. Fellows our housemaster that evening when he administered punishment to all for pillow fighting in my dorm…..even though I had kept out of it. A black and blue arse put me in hospital was the result. Ever seen the film Young Winston. Well, that happened to me in my 1950s. My head bashed against the blackboard by my math's teacher for not understanding an equation was not the least of the brutality I suffered from the teaching profession at that time. School days. Happy days? Not bloody likely! I hated them! And rightly so as I saw them.

Catterick living as a young Tom in 1964? Hairy, sweaty and smelly most decidedly! If you have never been in a barrack room with twelve farty arsed, aggressive, profane, argumentative, occasionally vomiting drunken young men then thank the Lord, you have been blessed. On top of it all was the discipline, from day one. Being screamed at by psychotic corporals and sergeants. It didn't matter what you did it was always wrong! They screamed anyway!

You made your bedding into a bed pack at 6am, sheets and blankets folded neatly into a box shape, brasses were shined, blancoed webbing laid out, block cleaning and floors polished with a 'bumper.' Christ! We would have made handy little house-maids, we polished everything that didn't move!

Then the three s's: shit, showered and shaved before breakfast by 7am, dressed and into the kit required for the day's activities as per the programme. Galloping back for changes of clothing two or three times during the day, (known as change parades), weapons training, PT, drill, more training, more drill and so on until you felt dead beat at the end of it all. Not quite. Bulling boots could take half the night. Spit, polish, and 'spooning' boots to smooth out the leather dimples, flattening them with a hot spoon, heated on a candle. We were meant to be volunteers for the new army of the sixties but somebody hadn't read the script it seems. These buggers were still in conscription mode. Take pay parade for example. Now if your name was Archer or Brown, you could be quaffing ale in the NAAFI, (Naval Army Air Force Institute), the providers of shops and services bars to the troops, before the Walters or the Youngs had even received their pay. Alphabetical order was the same in the army as we had been used to in school, never starting at the end, just for fairness the odd time, but no it never happened. After one week of this mayhem Betty Windsor, (the Queen), dropped me a fiver. A whole five pounds! Well, stap me vitals! Five quid and all my own. Well not quite.

Once I'd got my fiver from the pay clerk, I passed down the table to the next in line and so on until after: sports fund stoppages, barrack room stoppages, damages and more damages, haircuts, etc. etc. I was left with less than £4. But as a pint in the NAAFI was about 1/- and I didn't drink and I had my savings already booked into my POSB, a Post Office Savings Book, which I was sending home on a regular basis to my mother. This lasted for the next four years whilst I was overseas, mum always got my remittances, until I got married. Memories of Catterick? It wasn't so bad really. I found out I was a x-country runner, when I came second behind an army champion, and he ran with spikes whereas I only had slippery army issue plimsolls. Trouble is that sort of thing gets you noticed. I think the OC had had a bet on me for the garrison event and as bad luck would have it, after training up for two weeks, the night before was our intake piss-up in Richmond. Guess who was sick and spewing up for the best part of the run? The OC wouldn't talk to me after that. I did finish though....20th or thereabouts ...I think.

I had another runner who trained with me, trooper Ryan and we jogged along quite comfortably, little did I know Ryan, the Army regime was slowly sending him crazy and one day he went completely off his rocker.

It began one bleak morning as we were readying for the day and our Corporals were chivvying us to get a move on. Such as, "GET A FUCKING MOVE ON YOU IDLE BASTARDS!" Delivered *sotto voce* by these brass lunged NCOs. Ryan however sat on his bed and they screamed at him in unison, all to no avail, he wouldn't budge. The Intake Sergeant hove into view and took in the scene rather calmly, I thought.

"Ryan, he said quietly, "are you going to get dressed or not?" "No. Replied Ryan. "I'm refusing to soldier and won't wear any uniform ever again!"

So, saying, Ryan scragged his locker and began throwing all of his kit around the barracks as well as out of the windows. Well. Our Sgt. took this insubordination in his stride. "March Ryan to the guardroom," he ordered.

Hurriedly one of the NCOs marched us way from this scene of confrontation and blatant disobedience, ... just in case it spread like the pox and others became infected. Ryan ambled off to the guard-room, escorted by a L/Cpl., who was nearly having a fit as he tried to march Ryan to the clink.

Later we heard Ryan had attacked the M.O in his office and had to be pried off the doctor, who wisely, once two orderlies had held Ryan down, put him out with an injection. Ryan was then bundled into an army ambulance and whisked off, unconscious to the military hospital at Netley, near

Southampton. The psychiatrists probably had a field day peering into what brain cells Ryan could display.

Poor sod! We never heard of him again and no doubt he was turfed out of the army in due course. Shame really because he was a good x-country runner!

Where was I when Kennedy was shot in November 1963? Out on the moors on exercise, cold, wet and hungry when I heard the news. Just before my compo meal of tinned bacon and beans.

Personally, I couldn't have cared less. All I wanted at that time was to get dry, warm and fed, stuff the politics, and stuff some Yankee President who couldn't keep his head down and his flies done up! And in all of my years since I haven't changed one bit. Politicians of today such as, Blair, Corbyn, Cameron and slime such as Gerry Adams are all of the same low pond life as the Kennedy clan…. I'd cheerfully lock up the fucking lot of them. My last training exercise in Catterick was in December 1963, in cold, wet and bloody freezing conditions. However, I did know the area, having been brought up as an army brat when my dad was posted there in the fifties. Part of this army brat knowledge was knowing where the live .22 rounds were dropped on the ranges after the troops had been firing on the FMR, the Firing Miniature Range, and being technically minded and industrious, my play-mates and I dug these rounds up and squished them between two house bricks. Then with another brick we bashed the rounds at the blunt end, knowing that they were rim-fire and they would go off with a satisfactory bang. How the hell we never shot each other I don't know…but it was fun. Thinking my local knowledge of the area would be an advantage I volunteered for a night patrol.

This night patrol was led by a clot of a corporal and it blundered into and was captured by *'the enemy side'*. Bollocks to this I thought. I wasn't having any of it and pushing an opponent to the ground I made a break for it ………and in the dark and after the hundred-yard dash, tripping over tussocks …. I ran straight over the edge of a quarry! I dropped for a few feet and rolled down slope some 20 feet and miraculously bounced up to run onto my HQ; reporting on the wood where the enemy were concentrated. A pat on the back for my escape and front-line intelligence about the enemy would have been nice, maybe?

Nah! Little good it did me as my first Christmas in the army saw me on guard duty at Catterick Camp watching on as everyone else either went on leave or tucked into their turkey dinners in the cook house. Being chosen for guard was simply because of not being an NCOs favourite or a pal. A refrain from WW1 came to mind as I peered into the lit windows of the messes, as all about me got beastly drunk and got stuffed on turkey to boot!

(Sung to Tidings of Comfort and Joy)

It was Christmas Day in the cook house, the happiest day of the year,

Men's hearts were full of gladness and their bellies full of beer.

When up spoke Private Short House, his face as bold as brass, saying,

"We don't want your Christmas pudding; you can stick it up your arse!"

It was Christmas Day in the hareem, the eunuchs were stood around,

with hundreds of beautiful women laid on the ground.

When up strode the big bold Sultan, gazing about his marble halls, saying,

"What do you want for Christmas boys?" And the eunuchs answered, "Balls!"

The CO of the 3RTR Training Regiment at that time, I don't know his name, but he had the decency to walk with me as I patrolled a wet and windy guard duty, with my pick helve, in Catterick Camp on Xmas Day 1963. All I had to look forward to was a cold congealed plate of Xmas dinner laid on in the guardroom after my 'stag' on duty was over.

Part of the time I snuggled up to the warm air coming from various outlets. (Sentries always seem to get nobbled in every Hollywood film you will ever see. (Not surprising really because they were always trying to hideaway to get warm!)

A black and white photograph of our passing out parade intake 63/20 appeared recently on Facebook and before long several people on that photo wanted a reunion. Now I don't know about you but just think about this. We met for the first time when in our teens and twenties. The oldest bloke was 25 and he was nick-named *'Pop!'* We got on for about 12 weeks and that's about it.

One friend of mine George, who went to the 4th Royal Tank Regiment kept in touch as he went to Brunei & Aden and I went to Hong Kong, Libya & Cyprus, but that dropped away as it always does over time.

Now 50 years later someone wants to reminisce? About what? What did you do in the army after you left Catterick? How have the years treated you?

Are you dead yet and if not, who do you know who's dead? Oh. Bugger off! Pass the G&T I'm out of here…! Maybe I'll write a book instead.

The tank park at Catterick in 1963.
The Main barracks, Cambrai and Alma are in the back-ground.

HAVING BEEN A SOLDIER

After pass-out parade 63/20 intake in December 1963. Alma Barracks. Catterick Garrison. Interesting that Alma was chosen for an RAC /Cavalry barracks name...considering Alma was a battle fought in the Crimea by the PBI and the cavalry was kept in reserve! Blame all to the Commander Lord Raglan who insisted that the cavalry was, "To kept in a band box." This just before the massacre of the Light Brigade in the 'Charge of the Light Brigade and the dusting up of the Cossacks cavalry by the Heavy Brigade. Such is history made.

CHAPTER 2

TIDWORTH AND SQUASHED TOES

Tidworth is an army garrison in the south of England, probably dating from the 19th century and possibly before. Tacked onto the bottom edge of Salisbury Plain it is ideal country for tank and infantry training. Let's face it there aren't many places in the UK where tanks can race about and churn up the countryside. And of course, the MOD, Ministry of Defence jealously guards its territory. There were and still are villages and hamlets cut off and abandoned by the inhabitants from the war years, used as a training area even today. Imber for one. Surprisingly for all of the military activity, the Plain is a wild life oasis where even after live firing exercises by the artillery and tanks, life amongst the animal inhabitants goes on quite normally.

Salisbury Plain Training Area.

Rare species survive because interfering civilians are kept out. I've seen this phenomenon in later years, particularly on Hohne ranges and Soltau training areas in Germany and in Suffield in Canada in the seventies and the eighties. Live firing training areas such as these keep tourists out. Says it all really as they are the real despoilers with their huge numbers, their families, their cars, their motels, their Mac D's and their loud noise, their demands and their litter. Paul Theroux makes this point in his book *'The Happy Isles of Oceania.'* A travel writer he meets says of the islands of the Pacific, as they speak of her work, "Three hundred years of colonialism have done less harm to the world than thirty years of tourism."

The odd Battle Group, firing as they go is a mere pinprick when stacked up against modern tourist demands on open spaces.

Take where I live today. The English Lake District in Cumberland. Whole areas are being despoiled by local government, councils, tourist agencies and other do gooding bodies such as the world heritage bureaucratic agency and its, "We are here to help" interference ...and that's before the litter louts of the 'Townie,' tourists arrive to make the place a shit hole. Hell! There are so many brasher boots grinding the hills down that soil erosion is a constant threat. The ancient hills of Cumbria that withstood the Glaciers of 10,000 years ago are being eroded by feet, thousands of *'anoraks'* marching up and down, wearing away the hillsides. These very same people complain about low flying RAF fighters practicing their low flying skills, spoiling their day in the hills!

A few RAF bombing raids would clear the bloody lot out and the farmers, sheep, foxes and badgers could live in peace ever after.

But only so long as they used their fox hounds and hunted down and killed off all of the bureaucrats and civil servants in the National Trust and other agencies.

So here I am posted to Tidworth, in an Irish Regiment for all of two days. As I hadn't had any Christmas leave my good and kindly troop Sgt Rock sent me off on 10 days leave! (Forget the good and kindly- Sgt. Rock proved to be a martinet!) But actually, he wasn't, he was just doing his job, and years later I actually felt some affection for the old bugger...he wasn't too bad....as sergeants go! The troop I was assigned to was a typical mix of Irishmen, southern and northern, I was the only Englishman in the troop, apart from some of the NCO's who lived outside in married quarters.

Comrades? The odd dig in the back of the head on the tank park, delivered for no reason tended to concentrate one's perception on the mores of conduct amongst the Irish. "Why did you do that?" Usually elicited the response, "Because I felt like it, you English *twat!*"

My first falling out was with a Belfast bully, who along with a drunken pal dragged me out of bed for a fight in the early hours of the morning at Castle Martin ranges in Pembrokeshire. Deciding I'd had enough of this low-level bullying and intimidation, I offered to fight them both, walked out and was immediately decked from behind by a well-placed house brick in the back of the head. So much for comrades.

Tidworth was where I got my first two 'charges.' The first was when arrived back from a day's exercise to find I was slated for guard duty that night. Lo! And behold I was charged by the inspecting officer, with hair down to 'his' collar, for not appearing on guard duty with a haircut. Squadron Orders and a £2 fine. This was followed by a Lance Corporal ordering everyone out of bed and charging the whole room with disobeying a direct order when we failed to comply. Power mad of course, as all LCpls. were.

It is a fact; give anybody a uniform, traffic wardens, police, train staff, anybody, and the certainty is that they will abuse and brow-beat their un- uniformed citizens mercilessly. Adolf Hitler knew this and any camp guard at Auschwitz would recognize a fellow soul-mate in the average parking warden or policeman of today. "Just following orders, you know. Now move along, nothing to see here!"

Another £2 fine! I didn't know that these first charges at Squadron level would be my lot until I had collected three pages. Most of them being trivialities, such as swearing in mixed company, using a fire-bucket to wash the ablutions, stealing a bus, fighting and being D&D. Then when I made sergeant, they were all annulled.

My Centurion tank crew were a different story. I had Cpl. Jones as commander. B.J as gunner and Mac as the driver.

I, Geordie was the new loader/radio operator. I couldn't have had a better trained crew in the squadron……they were also the three biggest alcoholics in the regiment. B.J. had a working still in his locker and under his bed he was stuffing apples/potatoes and anything else he could get his hands on. He had the fermentation jugs and bottles there to feed the bloody thing. I had heard he had even tried distilling boot polish and tank anti-freeze to extract alcohol! On exercise, everywhere I turned in the tank turret there were cans and cases of beer. The ready round lockers had no room for projectiles or ammunition, they were filled up with stacked up beer cans. I had never ever heard of a seven pint 'party can' until this moment. But it fitted a ready round bin perfectly!

I had to sit with live 20 pounder AP rounds on my lap on battle runs because there wasn't enough space to fit them in. The commander used to threaten me with death if I so much as looked at the safety switch which stopped the turret traversing when I had to reach forward to grab rounds from the for'rard lockers. Naturally he wanted full traverse to engage targets, bugger the poor loader if he lost his arms in the process! Having said that, Cpl. Jonesy was the commander I wanted to be. He knew his job and he was very good at it. If you had had to go into a tank battle, he, B.J & Mac were the best, professional in their different skills.

A live battle shoot at Castle Martin.

I was loading …. three rounds of 20 pounder AP … at 800 yards…at 1000 yards and 1200 yards in six seconds proved that. Target! Target! Target! With its flat trajectory and a speed of over 1700 yards per second the armour piercing Sabot round was something the poor tankers of WW2 could only have dreamt about. With the turret traverse safety switch turned off, my only safety was the loaders shield, a retracting plate that I yanked shut as I shouted, "Loaded!" And this was the only thing between me and a recoiling one-ton breech block as the gunner fired. BANG! The plate slammed back with the breech as a smoking brass case was ejected into the bread basket.

I rammed in another 20-pounder round with its brass case, shut the breech and closed the guard plate… BANG! Another round went off. Already I was shoving the next round into the breech, Clang! It shut! BANG! the shoot ended after three rounds. The smoke, the smell of cordite, the explosion, the violence projected, the yells of the crew, my screams of 'Loaded', in response to the commander's orders to 'Fire' and the gunners 'Firing now!' Unless you have done that, you haven't a clue of how it feels.

The excitement, the exhilaration, the power!

We also lined up the squadron on the Castle Martin ranges, all 16 tanks and loaded canister rounds.

A line of targets was set out. A couple of hundred figure of 11-man targets were presented.

Canister was an anachronism from an earlier age but it was still there in 1964. A black tin can filled with 200 steel pellets.

Apparently, it had been brought back in Korea to sweep clear massed Chinese troops swarming over our tanks. *BANG!* The bloody lot was fired on a word of command. Sixteen guns firing two hundred steel pellets in each can and the canister at a range of one hundred yards disintegrated all of the targets to our front. Shades of Wellington and his forlorn hopes in similar circumstances in 19th century battles. The range was 100 yards, a killing range for the PBI. (Poor Bloody Infantry.) But for tanks? The Germans were knocking out our tanks in WW2 with their Tigers at 1000 yards plus with 88mm cannon. In those days we still had poxy 75mm Sherman's or Churchills that couldn't hit a house at that range.

OK there was the 'Firefly', a Sherman with a 17 pounder, much later. And if it did hit the shell bounced off their armour unless at close range.. No wonder we loved the Centurion. So did the Israelis. They used Cents better than we ever did, in the last years of the war, in Korea and Suez in the 50's. Best tank ever they said and they knew how to use them in their wars against the Arabs in their Russian T34s & T54/55s in the desert tank battles of 1948, 1956 and later in 1967.

Battle exercises in a Centurion

For the technically minded. The Sabot round had a 'dispersing' shoe i.e., *'sabot'*, held in place by a nylon driving band, which fitted the bore of the gun. When fired the driving band was ripped off and the shoes fell away in the first second of firing, then the inner projectile made of tungsten steel went on its way at over 1700 ft./sec. The result when it hit a hard target was awesome. A 50-ton tank at 1000 yards away could be lifted off its tracks and blasted to smithereens, so of course were the crew. End of technical stuff. BJ had a poacher's skills for night time forays to supplement our field rations. As we leaguered up for the night in a 'hide.' He would creep out into the nearby woods with a hollow antenna rod and threaded wire fed through it with loop at the end. Shining a torch into the lower branches I would pin-point a roosting pheasant and BJ would slip the noose over the unsuspecting and blinded bird and yank it out of the tree. The next day as we roared over the plains, our tank would be issuing clouds of feathers out of the turret as I plucked our nights catch. That evening, with a can of cold beer each and a roasting pheasant on a slow burning fire, who could have been happier? And we were being paid too!

Following any exercise on the Plain the tanks had to be washed down. High powered water jets and wet, mucky work followed as we physically had to dig the hardened mud off the suspensions and tracks. I was doing just that, my head under a track supported by top rollers and digging away at an idler wheel when the tank was moved! With the engine running I'd not heard any changes and with a foot under the track they said I could have been heard in Sidbury Circle, about half a mile away. As the song around at that time was "Baby love where did your love go?" It didn't take long before BJ was singing, "Geordie love where did your toes go?" Followed by, "Under the tracks dear!" Very funny. Not so funny was the board of enquiry where my testimony, given truthfully and without any malice didn't do Cpl. Jones' future promotion prospects any good, he being responsible for moving the tank without checking it was clear to do so. I suppose I was lucky it was only my left foot; it could have been my head under the idler wheel. I did feel guilty about Jonesy though. After asking nurse Kalazinsky in the Tidworth Hospital to marry me and being summarily rejected, I went off on sick leave, limping around my home town Wallsend on Tyne like a stricken warrior. One night with a couple of girls at The Metal Bridge in Gretna I got very drunk. My poor old 'Nana' whom I was staying with, got blitzed on her favourite Rum & Pep and I spent the night with the two girls all three of us in one bed ...and nothing happened we were so pissed! Bloody hell!

Not that I didn't try! But they were passed out.

Once back at Tidworth it was all preparation for The Enniskillen Parade. In 1964. It was a scunner. I have spoken to others since then on this parade and they all remember as I do on the atrocious weather, rain and more rain. I don't know why it is but the powers that be like a parade. Ordinary squaddies don't. For a start off they have to bull their kit, polish and polish again. Then they get inspected, again and again. Troop sergeant's inspection, troop officer's inspection, Squadron Sergeants Majors inspection, R.S.M. Inspection, Adjutant's inspection…for Christ sakes who's next! God? It goes on and on until the final day of the parade when the King of the Belgians or the Sultana of Zanzibar says, "Zay look smart do zay not?" Whilst the RSM is grinding his teeth and muttering under his breath, "I'll *kill* that scruffy twat in C Sqn. front rank as soon as I can get my hands on his fucking scrawny carcass…. So, help me!"

The Congregation at the Cathedral.

And so, it came to pass. In pouring Fermanagh rain, the Regiment marched in its polished and over inspected finery up Enniskillen high street, leaving a trail of white Blanco down its pressed trouser legs and like a slug trail along the street, in the drenching rain, all the way to the Cathedral.

Once there, wet and miserable, thankfully they soon began to warm up, their soaked uniforms beginning to smell strangely like two hundred wet fox hounds

The cavalry officers and the King of the Belgians probably felt right at home with the familiar scent, turning around in the Cathedral and looking for their favourite hunter.

The ball that night, OK the dance. This is where the local girls get to grab any soldier worth the grabbing or where the ugliest soldier has a chance. I didn't get grabbed but I did meet Maria. I don't remember much but I do know that this girl was my first real romance. Naturally I boasted to my roommates that I had had the best shag of my life, to which they responded in loud guffaws, 'AdAway with ye..Catholic girls don't open their legs so easily.. bollocks you chancer!'

I'd tried earlier in Tidworth and had met a very fanciable girl but had made the mistake of cuddling her on a settee in front of her father. He naturally took offence at seeing his daughter mishandled in this way and forbade her to have anything more to do with 'low life soldiers'. Fair point.

Maria was, I learnt later a Roman Catholic, so what? Religion was an irrelevance I could do without it. Later her mum asked, that if I were to marry Maria, would I allow our children to be raised as Catholics. Of course, I would, it mattered not.

I returned later that year for my leave and after some heavy petting at her aunt's house, but no sex, I was night on night, frustrated... as we were both.

I couldn't fault her family's hospitality, her Ma' looked after me as an honoured guest, a full Irish breakfast in the front room and her Da' was a great drinking companion. He took to me and we spent many a happy day at the Catholic pubs and bookies in Enniskillen.

What transpired later in 1969 when the troubles broke out, I dread to think, me an Englishman wedded to a Catholic girl from Enniskillen.

I was *in love* but things panned out very differently over the next two years when we were apart and living on hopes and promises that faded over time.

I was posted to Hong Kong, Cyprus and Libya. For two years we wrote to each other, we were promised to be wed, that's how it was in those days. No mobile phone calls, no texts, no Skype. No instant contact.... just a letter every week or so. Ahhh! Those days were so very different. Yet I kept her photograph beside my bunk bed for the best part of two years, as promised and until .... well until Libya in 1967.

Before I left Tidworth, our regiment was tasked to go to RAF Lyneham to load baggage for our next-door neighbours, the Royal Scots who were crashed out to reinforce Aden, this yet another remnant of the Empire which was being defended to the last dead soldier by the political chancers of the period.

Labour or Conservative...take your pick.

But what an eye opener, the accommodation and messing at RAF Lyneham. At Tidworth we had to go to our army cookhouse, carrying a metal mug for tea and our KFS/diggers, we did get a plate for our food but at the table, condiments there were none, the plate had to be cleaned before it was handed back at the serving hatch. Here we were served by cheerful bonny lasses with a choice of food unheard of in an army cook-house. The tables had cutlery! Condiments and cups and saucers! Food could be ordered, fried eggs - "How do like yours done?" Plates cleared away by the girls. Our bunk-rooms designed for transits had carpets and were two-man rooms with wooden furniture instead of steel lockers and steel sprung beds. Bloody hell the RAF knew how to live and their women were a damned sight better looking than the tough looking arm-wrestling ground sheets we saw around our barracks. (Not true actually. I was posted to Bovington Camp at a later date and the WRAC there were decidedly very decent lasses; one I got to know well and my family and I still maintain contact with her 50 years later.) But at the time at Lyneham, I nearly deserted to re-sign on in the RAF!

With our next-door neighbours, the Royal Scots away in Aden it wasn't long before the OMO, *'On My Own,'* washing powder packets began to appear in the married quarters kitchen windows.

And the Irish lads didn't need any prompting. Military Police patrols spent a considerable amount of their time chasing trouser-less young men through the washing lines of the back yards of Sidbury Circle married quarters. One occurrence at that time springs to mind. My Dad had said when I joined, "Don't volunteer for anything!" Well, that's fine I say but, in the summer of 1964, there was a call for volunteers to be lifeguards at the family pool in Tidworth.

Who but a cretin would turn down such a job? So, there we were, me still recovering from my tank foot crushing incident and Sean Flynn from Dublin....God's gift in swimming trunks to frustrated females from the Royal Scots.

My first afternoon on duty. Sean sidles up to me with a woman of the female persuasion latched onto him and says, "Keep an eye out." And with that he and his partner disappear into the gents' changing rooms. Keeping my eye on the half-drowned toddlers I can't help but hear the squeals and the groans emanating from the changing rooms.

Funnily enough I never got any of this for the summer I was there. Perhaps it was because the married women of the Scots trusted me to look after their children or was it because they could smell a virgin at fifty paces and I wasn't considered a threat. Many years later when working offshore in the North Sea I had an obnoxious Scots Offshore Installation Manager, who told me he was born in 1965, to a Royal Scots in Tidworth. Now in his thirties it didn't seem diplomatic or wise to suggest to my boss that his parentage could have been fifty-fifty Irish and Scots. In fact, a bastard in more ways than one! Well!

The Empire. Going. Going. Gone!

Aden.
Looking towards Little Aden from Jebel Taalla 1964

Hong Kong Harbour 1964

Sarawak 1964- Kuala Bakam –

Libya 1966- Convoy led by a Saladin

CHAPTER 3

HONG KONG KAMTIN AND OTHER INCIDENTS

The fan overhead going thump thump all night long didn't do much to move or to disperse the heat that had built up during the day, all it did was to the cool any naked parts of your sweaty body that you were inclined to expose. Christ! It was hot! I woke up each morning with the smell of the night soil attendant moving the shit buckets from the latrines. Welcome to the exotic Far East! Complete in living colour and stink. Lying, sweating and stark naked under a mossie net, watching Gecko lizards run across the ceiling, and listening to the constant buzz of mosquitoes.

Our camp was Sek Kong Camp in the New Territories. An airfield at the bottom of the TWISK, Tsun Wan and Sek Kong, a hairpin of a road leading up to the Chinese border.

Squadron of Centurions lined up on Sek Kong airfield Hong Kong. Four troops of three tanks each and SHQ. Troop of two.

On the advance party in 1964 we were in the old camp whilst a new camp was being built across the airfield, hence the thunder-boxes and the night soil attendants. Stinky corner on our way into Kam Tin was where the shit buckets were emptied and the effluent raked over to dry it before the resultant fertiliser was bagged up to sell to pak choi vegetable growers.

Sek Kong was at the bottom of a flat plain, large enough to fit a small airfield, surrounded by mountains to three sides it was a supposed alternative airfield for army needs. Personally in the year I was there I never saw any air activity ..not surprisingly as it looked a death trap for anything but sopwith camels or helicopters.

Our local was in Kam Tin. A village of tin huts and shanties. We did have some problem with 'The Bamboo Boys' who picked on lone night drunks back from Kam Tin. Wullie a semi tamed Yorkie got his own back one night by setting fire to one of their hooches where they gathered. Whether any of these local thugs were roasted or not, Wullie simply grinned. The two bars in Kam Tin were either Skins or Field Regt. And many a battle was fought there. What is it that differing British Army units always find a reason to scrap? Bye the bye. They did.

Staggering back one night, under the influence of three or four Tiger beers I reached stinky corner and fell into the monsoon ditch next to the fertiliser pits. My mates helped me out, using bamboo poles to keep me at a distance and then back at camp they prodded me, using the same poles, into a shower. Personally, I have never eaten pak choi before then or since. Other memories include one night when we rustled an innocent water buffalo and forced it into the Sergeant Majors office. It then did what all cattle do and our dear SSM had conniptions the next day. No culprits were found nevertheless. On another occasion coming back from Kam Tin one of our group, (under the influence), got entangled in a barbed wire fence and started screaming that he was being attacked by a cobra! It took some time to calm him down and fisticuffs resulted before peace was restored. We were in 1964 at the start of the American involvement in Vietnam, and we had a VD lecture by the MO in the camp cinema.

Looking at some of his slides I would have thought VD was the least of our expected genital worries. For example, he showed us various carbuncles, sores and other nasties that we were guaranteed to get if we so much as looked at a Chinese girl. His *piece de resistance* was a slide of a girl who worked the streets of Wan Chai, propositioning Yankee sailors and marines. Her Modus Operandi was to lubricate her customers erection with water from a bottle. Saying *"I am clean Johnny. Me make you clean"* Damn right she was clean quoth the MO.

"That bloody woman has put more GIs in hospital than the fucking Viet Cong!

As Lesley Thomas wrote in his book 'The Virgin Soldier,' we had a lot to learn and the learning sorted them all out. virgins included.

But that wasn't to last for long, not in Hong Kong anyway.

The VD clinic was soon seeing new patients. Captain Fanshaw with his dose from a high-class $300 hooker picked up at The Hong Kong Hilton found himself sharing the waiting room with Trooper Roscoe Tanner with his $12 dose, picked up on a bicycle trip to a Fanling whore house.

As the saying went amongst the locals...." *All same, same Johnny, all same."*

Others however had other ways. For example, Arthur a truck driver who had a fair bit of lee-way and having access to transport, which we tank park soldiers were denied, was a frequent visitor to the 'Winky Wanky' bar in Kowloon, as he drove rations from Hong Kong each day.

Never ever having gone there myself, it doesn't take much imagination to work out what Arthur's extra curricula activities entailed.

But it does have a certain ring, does it not? Sums up Hong Kong bars rather neatly I thought. 'Winky Wanky' indeed!

Arthur was an aficionado of the sexual niceties of your average back street bar. He could list all of the bar girl's favourite routines. There was a woman who picked up coins with her vulva, (some evil types heated up coins with their lighters, just to see the reaction but this little cutie was wise to that stunt), she could also draw a string of razor blades from the same orifice; another who could insert a lit cigar between her labia and could then puff smoke at the punters. Another trick was for an agile dancer to insert ping-pong balls into her vagina and then, after handing out children's shrimping nets, fire the damp and warm balls for her eager customers to catch.

A free beer for every ball caught!

Even less salubrious was the 'Better Hole' in Fanling. A memorable night in the squadron was when a troop decided to go for a for a bicycle ride to the nearest shanty town brothel. A convoy of a dozen bikes set off. With drunken soldiers falling off and bodies strewn along the way and then trying to scramble back on, it was chaos for the poor bike riders. The British army retreat from Kabul in 1840 was handled better. Price was as follows: bicycle boy-transport, one dollar there … one dollar back.

A jump with a muscular female paddy field worker, which was as good as a wrestle with a Dobermann Pinscher, $10. A dollar in those days was 1/6d. Ten dollars, then, about .75pence today. And as one Scottish Corporal in the Military Police said as he raided this den of iniquity at a later date cried, "Get yous to feck! D'ya know ken this is a hoose of ill repute!"

And no, I didn't go there, the MO's warning slides were enough for me.

Anyway, I was too busy in Kam Tin chasing skirt.

I could see the way things were with the rest of the lads, getting pissed getting tattoos and getting a dose. Some of the tattoos were of the usual sort, Palm trees and the usual crap. But the odd oddball wanted something better. One lunatic had a pair of army boots tattooed on each arse cheek then added a pair of hands crawling out of his belly-button. As for me ..no way. I have always classed these skin decorations as low class and even today cannot understand the stupidity that modern women and men desecrate their skin. I blame the Ancient

Britons and their northern savage cousins…the Picts for this descent into a barbaric practice. These were the early days and so much for good intentions, which didn't last long but initially I wasn't going to go down the same road as my pals. No tattoos, no smoking, no whoring… but boozing, afraid so, because that was the only way to meet a bar girl buying her drinks all night. Each time you bought a beer for yourself, you had to buy a coke for the serving lass, it was her commission. So, 5 to 10 dollars a night was not unusual, considering a beer on its own was about one dollar, this was the way to penury and the poor-house. Pockets leaking my friend!

I was after a bar girl, and one in particular, Christine Chan who worked at the Ying Wa bar in Kam Tin, a small village about a half mile or so from our camp at Sek Kong. Now everyone who has been in HK will tell you that all bar girls are whores…this is not so. Sure, there were lots but the majority of the girls I and others met in the Ying Wa and adjacent bars were anything but whores. Without a word of Cantonese and with sheer persistence over a period of 3 to 4 months I did my darnedest to get that girl to come out on a date with me. It took that long… now would a whore have taken that amount of trouble…. I think not.

We actually did do some military work in the meantime. Apart from our daily slog on the tank park we got dressed up in Number 3 dress whites for the Governor's House guard or the Queen's Birthday parade in Hong Kong.

Queens Birthday Parade Hong Kong Stadium 1965

You can check up this on The South China Morning Post. Apart from the publicity photos of me doing guard duties for the Governor, this from one of my Irish compatriots was a stunner. He maintained that the crown on Queen Elizabeth on a HK dollar was incorrect. This made front page news! Conniptions all around. Comparing a modern Major's crown and a crown on a dollar seemed easy...but as someone more au fait with crowns. It was simple. King's crowns v Queen's crowns. Just goes to show you though, journalists are really quite thick. So then we went on camp, firing live rounds across the South China Sea and converting gunners from 20 pounder tank guns to Saladin 76mm peanut shooters. We did exercises, a troop at a time on the Laffins Plain training area. It was so small that only a troop of three tanks could operate there at any one time. Bivvying up one night, I learnt a lesson from our troop officer that I tried to apply in my next twenty years of service. As we all struggled to get comfortable for the night bedding down on the ground in our four blankets issued for this purpose, we were amazed to see our troop officer, calmly getting his collapsible bed into position.

Once satisfied as to its stability he opened his bags and began to lay out bedding, mattress, plump pillows and crisp white sheets. Snuggling down in his pyjamas he uttered the words that I remember fifty years later.

"Never forget gentlemen .... any fool can be uncomfortable!"

Centurion Mark 5 with 20 pounder main armament. On Laffins Plain Training Area HK.
Some of these tanks saw service in Korea in the 1950's; and transported to Hong Kong thereafter.

We also had to man some of the border posts overlooking the Hong Kong mainland Chinese frontier. One such post was Robins Nest.

High up in the New Territories. It had a commanding view over the border. The only way to supply it was via mule train. Yep! We had them too.

We of course had to crawl up, loaded down with gear and weapons. But once there it had a superb view across acres and acres of Chinese paddy fields on the other side of the border. A night of chaos was caused when Cpl. 'Dinger' Bell came into the post shouting, "They're invading! The Chinese they're invading! There're thousands of the buggers! Look! There's lights everywhere!"

We were stood to and scrambled for our kit and weapons and dashed to our positions…then looked. And sure, enough there were lights everywhere. Trouble was it was the fireflies mating season and our redoubtable Corporal Bell had panicked. He wasn't quite the same after that.

Between times, whilst I was spending time and money in this bar chasing skirt, other incidents occurred. Some I was involved in some not. After a particular bar room scrap when a loud-mouthed Aussie got bottled, I an innocent bystander was shoved head first into a juke box, another chap was laid out in some road works outside the bar and the Sikh Police came in and twatted everybody that was still standing with their bamboo canes.

Funny thing that, the Sikh police never bothered with arrests, big lads as they were they just weighed in, smashing everybody down. No complaints though.

Time for an Aussie Joke.

There was this Aussie DJ who liked to ask the listeners to join in his show. One morning he started by asking his audience to come up with a new word and to put it into a sentence.

"I've got a word," says his first listener, "Garn!"

"I've not heard that before," says our DJ. OK, please put your word into a sentence."

"Certainly," comes the reply. "Garn fuck yourself!"

Shock! Horror! The DJ shuts off the line and apologies profusely to his listeners. "Oh! My! Sorry about that folks, lets continue with another caller, shall we?" The programme continues.

Sometime later, another caller phones in.

"And what is your word please," the DJ says.

"Smee," is the reply.

"Smee? I've not heard that before," says our DJ. OK, please put your word into a sentence."

"Certainly," comes the reply. "Smee again, now Garn fuck yourself!"

The Redcaps and the American Shore Patrols on Hong Kong were always out for scalps on their crime sheets, those bastards just loved paperwork. A normal week-end in Kam Tin or Fan Ling was preferable to Hong Kong Island, this was because it was infested with The Yankee Navy. Thousands of the buggers from the 7th Fleet; and when they arrived prices of everything shot up accordingly.

A British squaddie with his miserable $80 a week couldn't afford to keep up with the Spams and their bankrolls.

Some didn't even try. There were of course plenty of crafty soldiers who latched onto the Yanks, not for their company, dummy, but for their generosity in buying round after round. And apart from the free drinks there was another less friendly reason for this fraternization, which was sometimes a quick 'mugging' in a side alley, where a drunken pfc. Wilbur Kowolsky or Billy Joe Gentry were relieved of their wallets.

On the odd occasion a Yank did make his way up to the New Territories, but this was rare. A long serving Trooper Green, who wanted to see Vietnam exchanged places with an American marine who didn't want to visit Vietnam. Morning parade was brought to a halt when this yank fell out of the ranks, mortal drunk. We knew he was there we just wanted to see what happened next. The poor bloody SSM nearly had a heart attack.

Meanwhile 'Dodger' Green was on an aircraft carrier ploughing into the Tonkin Gulf. I don't think he ever got to visit Vietnam, flown off when he was discovered he came back to Hong Kong in chains and was dumped in Stonecutters Island nick.

It seemed at one stage there were other folk desperate to get away from the British Army. I can understand why 'Kid' Lowes tried to in his own inimitable way. His problem was bullying by the same Belfast bully who had tried the same on me in Tidworth. But as I'd fought back so this little toe rag went for an easier target - the Kid. The lad couldn't fight back as I had done so things reached a climax. The Kid went down to Kam Tin stole a motor bike and roared off for the Chinese border.

This was at the height of the Chinese cultural revolution and when we went on patrol along the border the mad little buggers in their little green caps complete with a red star, dressed in ill-fitting green uniforms, barracked us and frantically waved their silly little red book at us. Loudspeakers bombarded us screaming and shouting Mao propaganda. "Imperialist, war warmongering, capitalist running dogs," and similar compliments were hurled at us courtesy of our highly agitated next-door neighbours. As for me and I don't know about the others, but two or three infantry battalions, one tank squadron, one gunner regiment, a couple of gunboats, a few RAF helicopters weren't going to cause the swarming Chinese infantry opposing us too much trouble; so hurling insults I could take, it was a damn sight better than hurling mass bayonet charges in my direction! Not that the Kid seemed to be too bothered. He drove through or around the several road-blocks layering the border area, several miles back from the border until he met the biggest and last chain link face complete with barbed wire and armed Chinese on t'other side. He did his Steve McQueen bit from 'The Great Escape', and piled right into the concertina wire. He was of course ripped up but as the amazed HK police arrested him and dragged him off, he was crying and in hysterics.

No gaol for the Kid. A psychiatrist had him sectioned and the last we heard of him was that he was sent to Netley to the Navy mental hospital near Portsmouth.

Our resident bully survived any backlash and the last I heard of him was that he subsequently murdered his wife at home in Belfast. So, he finally went to gaol…. pity it didn't happen sooner…before he killed his poor wife.

Another bully was Jack who was not only a bully but a real racist. Not something I had experienced to that date. He used to knock poor Chan, our room boy, about and demand money from the poor guy. This was a married Chinese of about forty years old, inoffensive and willing. I suppose this was the product of the Belfast slums, the lowest of the working class and determined to prove his superiority to the working class of Chinese.

This was something new to me. But then again, for a few he was a Chink, or a Wog, or a Spic or a Wop.

Today, racists; who blackened our good name throughout the Empire. Then again did we ever have a good name?

Gurkhas preparing to be-head a steer

Our local comrades, apart from the gunners were the Gurkha's and at their Dasheera festival we watched as they be-headed goats and cattle. It was indeed gruesome as they tied the bleating animal to a post; head tight against the post and legs straining against the pull, they presented a long neck for the Khukri blade. The steel blade was over two feet in length and with due dispatch sliced the head off the poor critter. It was unreal to see a steer, still standing before toppling over, a gap of several inches between head and body!

This was done in an open arena, sports ground and was the highlight of Dasheera. Later in the day the Gurkhas had their dances, which consisted of men dressed as women doing ethnic dances. And lots of beer. Good entertainers were the Gurkhas!

Much later I saw these same scenes, of beheading goats hidden from view in their barracks, instead of on the sports field. Times changed as PC took hold!

I have to mention our long-suffering sergeant major, SSM Raffles. He had a whole squadron of drunken, fighting vandals to deal with every week, never knowing what to expect next. A rustled water-buffalo shoved into his office late one night was the least of his problems. With the very near theft of a six-wheeled armoured car when a couple of drunks tried to steal it one night, and thankfully crashed it into the perimeter fence before legging it; this would have made the Kids escapade with a motor bike seem like child's play. It could have been an international incident if these two idiots had succeeded in getting as far as the border. No wonder the SSM wasn't well. He did his best though.

One thing that we all did was to visit our local tailor, Ah Lee. His establishment was just outside the camp gates, and we all ordered the best of Italian suits which were all the rage about then. We may have been drunken vandals but we were properly dressed hooligans for the occasion.

Suited up with white shirts and slim ties or with slacks and blazers we were the spivs we had always wanted to be. (Ah Lee was always generous with his tick book – order now- pay later.)

This I was to see some twenty years on when I re-visited Hong Kong as a tourist. Ah Lee was still in his tailor's shop when I called in. I mentioned that I had been a customer of his previously, way back in the sixties. "Ahh So! and who was your sergeant major then?" he queried. I mentioned SSM Raffles.

With that he went into the back of the shop and came back with an exercise book with Raffles' name on it. "The Ilish men," he said confidently, "Mr. Laffles." I had to admire his accounting, if not his pronunciation. My measurements for my suit made over 20 years previously were all detailed along with the fact that I had paid my bill, along with a few of whom I knew hadn't. I promptly ordered another blazer complete with my new regimental crest…. errm the measurements had changed in the meantime. In 2005 when I next visited, after the handover of Hong Kong to the Chinese his premises along with most of Sek Kong camp was no longer there. It was I suppose but it was desolate. The married quarters bungalows, the SKC, the Naafi were all boarded up, all gone…. history. It made me very sad, just as my if youth had passed away; which of course it had. There were others such as our room-boy Chan who folded our mossie nets, cleaned our room and cleaned our boots each day. We all paid him ten dollars each a week and some didn't cough up but borrowed from him as and when they were stuck for cash. Then there was Abdul and his sidekick from Pakistan who provided sandwiches on the tank park and late at night when the drunks came home to roost.

If you haven't tasted an Abdul sandwich at midnight then as an epicure you haven't lived!

He ran a tick book and there were some who borrowed from him too!

Cash was a problem with all of these out-goings that it was sometimes difficult to keep up with it all. Some did as the odd foray into civilized society proved. With his sharp new suit and cash in his pocket, Trooper Bob Fields and a pal were sinking beers in the Eagle's Nest in the Hong Kong Hilton with Matt Monroe as guest vocalist, when Bob invited Matt to join him. Apparently, they were from the same London borough – Bermondsey.

One thing led to another and Matt was invited to sing at the NAAFI club in Sek Kong. Of course, the army had to make the most of it and I and others met Matt on a publicity visit to the tank park, along with a fantastic free performance at our club where he sang his full repertoire. What a bloke. It was a shame he died in his prime. It would do some of the so-called singers of today who screech and wail, sticking their fingers in their ears and trying to reach a higher note, such as Adele, to listen to a good ballad singer.

I still play his records as often as I can, indeed as I write this, I have one of his LPs playing. He was a true gentleman.

Another visitor to Hong Kong was grabbed by the same means, Harry Seacombe. He too appeared at our club and performed as only a 'Goon' could, totally free and with no side to him at all...but what else could you expect from an ex-gunner from WW2.

Then there was murder. This was over Christmas when a taxi driver was found dead in his cab ...just outside Kam Tin. Myself and Ronnie had spent the Christmas with a married couple as their guests. However, when the cops decided to interrogate the whole British Garrison, (The poor taxi driver had been killed by Europeans it was claimed).

I was interviewed by the cops and I blithely stated that I had spent Xmas with no one else other than the family. Basically, leaving Ronnie on his own with no alibi and a suspect for a murder charge! All was sorted out eventually but he was not amused!

And talking of murder. Not long after that we were on patrol just south of Fanling and near to the burial grounds where some one million graves are situated that we came across a multiple murder. As the driver in a land-rover I spotted a body lying at the roadside and stopping, I got out to look. My NCO wanted to forget it and drive on, but I ignored the corporal and I went up to the body and could see he that had been shot in the chest. Some argument about not getting involved but I insisted and walked to an open bar in a hostile area and demanded that the bar tender called the police. The bar emptied rapidly once a "Gwailo", (European- Long nose), appeared and with reluctance and glowers he did so whilst my NCO squawked about getting out of there before we got shot! Walking about I spotted a car piled up in the foliage and looking closer spotted yet another body slumped over the wheel. He too was leaking claret from a gunshot wound to the head. Two killings! I wasn't going to walk away from this. With my corporal demanding that I get back in the Land Rover I was saved from any disciplinary action by a police Land-Rover turning up and a European officer taking control. His men fanned out and found yet another body hidden from view behind the car, all shot dead. It seemed, as he explained a gang turf war between rival gangs who wanted to control access to graves by relatives in their patch…hence the killings. After explaining that we had arrived on the scene after the murders he wasn't particularly interested in us as witnesses and to my corporal's relief we were sent on our way. Never heard anything about it after that! Odd, isn't it? Meanwhile my courtship of Miss Chan was reaching fruition. Many nights of visiting the Ying Wah bar was about to pay off.

Eventually I got her to meet up with me in Kowloon and after a day wandering HK harbour sight-seeing and after a Chinese supper, she had made the big decision, we booked into an hotel for the night …and that was it, a virgin soldier no more! Then of course I had to make a pig of myself. We had other nights in hotels. One night was most embarrassing for her when the police knocked on the door and demanded of her who I was. An afternoon on a hillside when a tiger was reported to be wandering in the New Territories and I was scared that my naked buttocks would end up as a tiger's breakfast. Playing the piano in the St. Andrew's lounge, Church of Scotland, when all had gone late at night, she seated on the keys whilst I stood with her legs wrapped around my waist; she wasn't very musical I must say, but jollity always won through as we played Chopsticks together. (Seen it in Pretty woman but I was there first!) Nights on the beach, fighting off mosquitos …Ahh! Those were the days! If I was only 20 again! There wasn't a week went by when I didn't see her and the inevitable happened, I got the poor girl pregnant. Worse followed…. for her this was a no no. Her family would never accept a "Gwailo" a long nose., a white man. She would not contemplate a marriage, she had to have an abortion. And being the innocent and stupid I agreed. Cost? $600. Where the hell on my meagre wages of $80 a week could I get this money?

I went to the Sqn. 2I/c for a loan, a Catholic for crying out loud! And borrowed the money for an abortion. God help me! I went with Christine to some seedy place in Mong Kok, Kowloon. I paid up and after the 'procedure' whatever it was I took her to a quiet hotel. She was sick and so was I. It was a horrendous weekend. We agreed that that was that, we wouldn't meet again, she was going off to Singapore to be with her family. And she did.

And then I did my stupidest thing. With my pal Patrick we spent a nasty afternoon getting drunk in Fanling hurling drained glasses into the fireplace at the 'Better Hole.' Kicked out and late at night we staggered up to the bus station for a bus back to Sek Kong. No buses were available and no taxis would take us. Patrick made the decision. He turfed a driver out of a convenient bus, I got aboard as the passengers who were already there began bailing out and we set off. A few minutes later I was for some unknown reason, unscrewing light bulbs from the ceiling fixings when we crashed. We certainly crashed. We were lucky not to have killed anyone but we ended up in Stone Cutters Island Jail nonetheless. My OC went ballistic…not surprising really as all of his hopes for me went west! Bang went any promotion prospects, indeed the OC put a block on any of my chances for the next nine months. The judge at my civil trial went further, damning me and my like, "You are a disgrace, you think that your barbaric behaviour is what this colony needs! You soldiers think that you can come over here and cause mayhem…. well, you bloody well can't!" I did think of Kipling during this rant, "It's Tommy this and Tommy that so chuck him out the brute but when the bullets start flying………." Still, I got no more than a reprimand, thanks to the Hong Kong police Inspector who stood on my behalf. The same Inspector who had seen my actions after the Fan Ling killings and I knew I had got off lightly as I hadn't actually crashed the bus. Shame was all. My flight out of Hong Kong not long after that on my twentieth birthday was a mixed blessing. I at least came out of there with no tattoos, no dose and still a non-smoker, but with my promotion prospects such as they were in tatters.

CHAPTER 4

LIBYA SAND AND DUST

Our next posting was to Libya. I liked Libya; I liked the desert. Can't say much about the people but those that I did meet I had no objections to.

After Hong Kong and a short break in England this is where I was and it suited me. Our base was just outside Benghazi; Wavell Camp, named after that great British soldier General Wavell who had trounced the Italian army in the 1940's. In our tanks we had a bracket which was used to clamp the gun breech from running back under breech pressure. This we called "the stop running back" …. or as the wags would have it, 'the Italian Officer'.

This is by the by, we had converted by then from Centurion tanks to armoured reconnaissance; Saladins, Saracens and Ferrets. The Salad Can had a 76mm gun, the Saracen was a six wheeled APC and with the Ferret two-wheeler was armed with a. .30 machine gun. Wavell Camp was a flat piece of desert scrub-land on the outskirts of Benghazi. The barracks accommodation was 'Twynolm' corrugated tin huts, laid out in a military fashion, a cinema, a NAAFI and a parade ground with vehicle parks and naff all else.

There were no women other than a few married quarters on the fringes and a perimeter fence enclosing the whole lot. Apart from a few squadron bars which opened up there was nothing to do except get pissed or play poker or get into fights. Benghazi itself had nothing to offer apart from some overpriced bars and night-clubs which only the highly paid oil workers could afford. Some families lived in the town and they frequented the families only Ace of Clubs NAAFI bar.

(More later. About the Ace of Clubs)

From the start I loved the wide open and dry open expanse of the Libyan desert. Quickly learning the navigation expertise needed to read a sun compass I took a driving patrol twenty miles from camp, heading for a distant oasis, hit it spot on and returned on a one-day exercise. Not bad for a trooper only just arrived. It was a bit of a shock a little bit later to learn that some of the officers had not learnt the same skills. On our first major exercise our troop leader, a young Lt. got us lost. The sun compass had two halves, northern and southern hemispheres, this poor Rupert got them arse about face. And instead of heading in the supposed direction had the troop going 180 degrees in the opposite direction...deep into the desert.

I as a simple driver mentioned this fact to my commander a Cpl. as I pointed out where the sun was on the horizon. But he went along with it, saying, "I'm sure he knows what he's doing."

Two days later and with us running out of fuel, water and food we were finally found by air reconnaissance and pointed in the right direction.

This Lieutenant later became a General.

And so on return to barracks we got our resident D.J on BFBS, (British Broad Casting Service,) to play, *"The Legions Last Patrol,"* which we thought was hilarious; not so a certain party in the Officers Mess!

Saladin Six Wheel Armoured Car. 76mm Gun and two .30 Browning's. In desert colours with hessian cam nets.

I was a driver of either a ferret scout car or as a Saladin driver. I disliked the Salad Can six-wheeler as it was always getting punctures on rocky ground. Sand tyres are useless on rocks!

Not having enough tyre spares we could fix this by turning it into a four-wheeler. By jacking up the centre wheels and inserting wheel nuts into the suspension struts we could 'lose' the centre wheels and had enough spare tyres to keep the beast mobile on four wheels.

Water was always a problem. It was always a relief to see the water bowser turning up after a day's hard running. More for the vehicles than we ever needed. We still used water-skins slung across the turrets, the wet skins kept cool even on the hottest days due to evaporation.

And on some days the heat hit 100 degrees Fahrenheit, with the nights dropping to freezing. So much for our four blankets which made our beds.

Everyone had their own answer to this problem. We nearly all dug a small pit and laid on the ground, some wrapped in a cocoon of their own making, some trying to get a little warmth from the engine decks. All to no avail. We always woke up bloody freezing, only to get cooked soon after when the sun came up. Waking up with Scorpion or some other similar critter was not unusual. Shaking your boots out before putting them on was a must. The daily chores such as even taking a dump had its drawbacks …as my commander discovered as he squatted behind a convenient shrub. "Snake" He hollered as he ran back, trousers around his legs. We investigated and dug out a rather irate reptile. A quick whack with a spade ended this creature's life as it poked up from its hole and after I had skinned it, I wore a snakeskin hat band for the rest of that trip!

Later I found myself as the squadron 2/ics driver in a MK1 ferret scout car. Now with no turret this bugger could shift, 60 miles per hour was its top speed on dusty roads, a real flyer on the roads such as they were. We did fly! Every time I dropped the captain off at his house his good lady had the courtesy of saying to me as I dropped off his baggage, "Thank you for seeing my husband safely home." He too later became a General. Although when I reminded him of this at a reunion much later, of our earlier association, he blanked me and had a sudden lapse of memory? Why is I that I wonder? Do Generals regularly forget the men who saw them as mere junior officers?

Talking about flying. My officer had a thing about hunting, not unusual in a cavalry regiment. So, I wasn't too surprised when he introduced a hawk into our ferret scout car. It sat perched on a breeze block behind my driver's seat, hooded and quiet, so I didn't pay it any mind as we drove away.

We leaguered up and it was time to feed the bird. A bedou appeared from nowhere, as they do, and I swapped a can of army biscuits for a scrawny chicken. He prized the tin with a handle on it more than the biscuits.

A mate, who was a butcher in civvie life, diced the chicken and I swung a chicken leg about my head on a length of D10 wire to attract the falcon resting on my officer's arm. Nothing doing, the bird refused the bait. I did feel rather silly at my antics and my mates were crying with laughter as I swung the leg in ever faster circles, trying to tempt the bloody bird to launch itself at its dinner. End of which we fed the bird by hand and we ate the rest of the chicken ourselves. The hawk escaped and flew away the next day in disgust.

The following days saw us in a 'Ghibli' a sandstorm, and that was like living in a sandpaper environment. Dust and sand, you could eat it was that thick, and water was at a premium. But when it blew over …the skies were clear and you have never seen such clarity as you lay down at night, cold in your blankets on the ground and stared at the heavens and the stars. Bliss!

Following a gunnery camp near Aghedabi we had a serious incident. Whether it was a due to an unexploded WW2 mine or a mortar we didn't know. But as some chaps were clearing rubbish from the area, parachute flares and spent cases and other detritus they stood around the pile of rubbish. Someone it is believed kicked the fin of an unexploded mortar/mine and there was one hell of a bang.

I was stood next to my Ferret minding my own business when I heard this *CRUMP!!* and saw a puff of smoke and grit and bodies flying in all directions. Shocked, I grabbed our first aid kit from the Ferret and ran to the scene. There were over a dozen men on the ground, most in shock and all in a serious bloody mess. My first casualty I turned over was shredded across his back, he was torn up, blood-soaked shirt in rags. But still speaking. "Fuck off and leave me alone." He grunted. "I'm OK." I then went to another chap who was groaning. Looking at him I hadn't a clue were to put a field dressing as he looked as if his guts were about to come out. Thankfully others turned up and as I plonked field dressings where I could, others turned up who knew what they were about. My bodged efforts where soon laid by the wayside. And after all the blood and guts no one died from this incident. Fourteen men were injured but none died. So much is owed to the medics and casualty evacuation of the British Army…..as I was soon to find out myself personally.

Ferret Mk.2 Scout Car. Kitted out for the desert. Sand Channels, cam netting made of sand coloured hessian and water skins. Hanging on the sides they were kept cool as water evaporated.

After desert exercise we had little else to do and that of course led to trouble, usually kicked off by alcohol. My next visit to the Medics followed a poker weekend when I had got enough cash to buy a couple of crates of Amstel for a party and I got into a row with a room-mate.

I offered him outside and being as stupid as before, as in Castle Martin, I walked out and was immediately decked by a steel bucket in the back of the head. *(will I never learn...don't turn your back on an Irishman!).* Much blood later and the MO stitching me up without anesthetic, I had my own you see, provided by the Amstel Brewery! I went to bed, cursing all and sundry. All forgotten the next day. Indeed, I spent a night a few years ago at a reunion with my assailant and we had a good yarn about those days.

At about this time I volunteered for the SAS and once accepted I went into training, running the camp perimeter daily, sometimes accompanied by my troop officer who also wanted to keep fit.

He always swore afterwards that I was a mean runner and he meant it...I was determined to get into the SAS. One weekend I packed 50lbs of sand into a rucksack and set off on a run and nearly got arrested as a smuggler. My route was along the main Benghazi – Tripoli Road which by-passed an Arab police barracks where there was a check-point, presumably to prevent smuggling by long-distance lorry drivers. At the barrier I showed my ID card and passed through. I had just resumed my trot when a police car came out of the barracks and two grinning officers asked if I wanted a lift to the next town, about 100 kilometers away. I declined the offer as it wasn't on my itinerary. That was a mistake. They had obviously thought I was a hitch-hiker - and no hitch-hiker refuses a lift on the desert road. They were instantly suspicious. Their grins vanished and they demanded to know what I was carrying- mainly by gesticulating in a threatening manner which even my hazy knowledge of Arabic couldn't misinterpret. Already a large curious crowd had gathered to watch the fun. Sheepishly I opened up my bag of sand. The two policemen couldn't believe their eyes.

They looked at the sand, then at me, then at the sand again. I tried desperately to make them understand I was carrying sand because I wanted to keep fit. I struck poses and generally tried to demonstrate which muscles I was attempting to nurture. There was much shaking of heads, with pitying looks usually reserved for the feeble-minded, and a lot of muttering, presumably about mad dogs and Englishmen.

Eventually someone saw the joke. There was an Englishman caught by the customs attempting to smuggle 50lb of sand- and not good quality stuff at that- out of a desert country. The crowd howled with laughter. The police, laughing as hard as the rest, gleefully, sent me on my way. I trotted off with what dignity I could muster. Then when I was out of sight, I dumped my load of sand where it belonged. In the desert!

Sometime in 1966 I and a pal Dave set off to hitch hike to the American Airbase in Tripoli a few hundred miles up the coast from Benghazi. We did it, and in true British form, got arrested by the Libyan police for being vagrants, met many drunken lorry drivers and were very nearly refused entry by the Yanks when we arrived at our destination.

All good stuff and all good training. Apparently, the British were not welcome in the town of Sirte where we ran afoul of the police, they had long memories, and we were held responsible because the British had bombed the town during WW2.

At this time all sorts of "Adventure Training" was in hand, apart from Dave and I on our lone expedition, others were on the move exploring the western desert. Whenever the British Army gets bored, Adventure Training takes hold.

In this instance the call was Khufra Oasis. During WW2 Khufra was a LRDG base for attacks on the Germans. So, what could be more apposite than a long-range expedition south into the desert to Khufra?

Slogging through sand has its good points on Blackpool beach with kiddies and buckets and spades but day in and day out, digging 3-ton vehicles out of cloying sand is not to be recommended, particularly in temperatures of 100oF.

The highlight however of these expeditions was the discovery of an American Liberator bomber.

This bomber, "The Lady be Good", was last heard of on a mission over southern Italy in 1943 and disappeared thereafter.

LADY BE GOOD — IIND WORLD WAR BOMBER FOUND IN THE LIBYAN DESERT — 1966

The Lady Be Good in 1966

Discovered in the early sixties by an oil company, the bomber was smashed up but still recognizable minus the crew. Some papers found at that time on site suggested that the crew took off into the desert and were never heard of or seen again.

There was also a booklet on *"Survival in The Arctic!"* It would seem that this crew had happily bombed somewhere in the Med and then flew onto Libya, forgetting to stop at the coast and flew on, deep into the desert and on into oblivion.

So, our intrepid adventurers decided to do, as any adventurers would do… to put the 'plane back together again. Dragging wings about to make a 'plane shape they busily sorted it out. (This was before "The Flight of the Phoenix") movie. Unfortunately, there wasn't a gifted German aeronautical designer available to rebuilt it and so it remained a bag of nuts and rivets for future generations to gawp at. But you get the idea!

CHAPTER 5

CYPRUS AND THE UN

At his point I was posted to Cyprus, to relieve some of our chaps who were with the UN, allowing them to go on leave. So, I was now in the UN forces trying to prevent Greeks and Turks from massacring each other. Well, it had stopped them murdering unarmed British women out shopping, or ambushing & shooting British soldiers as they had done up until then. They had got their Independence a few years earlier and then began chopping each other up as they fought for control of the Island. A typical outcome as the British Empire was handed over to the local brigands and bandits and chancers, such as Makarios posing as politicians but engaging terrorists for their own greasy and venal ends. Much like our own politicians of course.

The blue beret and the UN fancy badge with the blue scarf did look well with neat shirt and khaki trousers but it didn't cut the mustard with the local girls nor with the locals. They were shooting at each and every one on a daily basis, blue berets included.

A Ferret Scout Car with the UN in Cyprus 1966

The first time I went on patrol I was handed a revolver and six bullets and was told, "Don't load the pistol, keep the bullets separate." I was amazed. Stuff that I thought. I'd seen a news photo of a scout car held at gunpoint by an insurgent on the scout car holding a gun at the commander's head and that was the last thing that was going to happen to me....so I loaded the .38 revolver and kept it by my side for the rest of my tour of duty with the UN. Not that it was ever needed. Later this same British UN patrol was between a Greek village and a Turkish village when a fire-fight between the two villages started.

High velocity rounds were flying overhead and when a few mortars landed close by was when the patrol commander decided to vacate the vicinity. So, the UN legged it whilst the Greeks and the Turks fought it out. No wonder the UN forces were regarded as useless. Can't fight and not allowed to fight, what use are they.

Sadly, we did have a few casualties and the worst was when a popular young officer was killed when his Ferret scout car overturned on a mountain road. After my tour was over, I handed back my six bullets and my revolver…. unused. Today in the 21st century, Cyprus is still an armed camp for all of its tourist attraction. Turkish, Greek, Cypriot, British and UN soldiers are still there, all pointing guns at each other. Nothing new in that I suppose.

I was sent by post a UN medal, much later, but not sure if I can wear it as I hadn't completed the requisite 90 days in Cyprus. I suppose if I'd been shot on any day during my service that wouldn't count either.

My next tale now goes to Hereford, to the SAS. With high hopes I joined in August 1966 what I supposed would be the highlight of my career.

Some hope. The SAS have a simple strategy, weed them out and it works.

Day one is an easy cross country run in full pack and weapon over the Brecon Beacons, a hilly mountain bog-land in Wales. It goes in stages, day by day starting at day one at 5 miles to 20 miles a day by the finish. No problem for fit young men.

Fit you might be but on day one I turned on a tussock of grass at full speed, fell, and broke a bone in my foot. That night I strapped up my foot and lacing up my boots on to keep the swelling down I tried to bluff day two but to no avail, I couldn't run with a busted foot.

Sympathy all round and "come back next year," as the Doc. said as he plaster-cast my foot. So that ended my SAS experience.

Only later did I get back in, into working alongside the SAS in Northern Ireland with Int & Sy Group and The Dets. – but that's a lot, lot later! What next…a posting to a holding unit at Bovington Camp in Dorset before I could be sent back overseas to my unit in Libya. Bugger! All that running and training for nothing and RTU'd to boot! (Returned to Unit.)

CHAPTER 6

BOVVIE CAMP

Bovington Camp in Dorset was the Royal Armoured Corp HQ. My father had spent most of the War years here as a tank instructor and it is where my brother was born in 1944. So here I was, an invalid hopping about on a pot leg waiting to be posted back to my unit overseas.

As a certified signaller and definitely useless in a mobile capacity I was given a desk job for the first time in my life, I became the Officers Mess switchboard operator. Bloody hell! Why me? Still, it had its upside, lots of time off and a chance to meet up with some of the WRAC girls.

One of whom I mentioned earlier who lived in the barracks above my room. I regularly sent her my shirts for ironing and she returned her shoes for polishing, all by way of strings dangling from floor to floor…neat don't you think. There was no thought of any hanky panky as she was already engaged and it was just friendship as 50 years later, we are still in contact as families.

Meanwhile I had visited my brother and borrowed ten pounds from him to buy a car. Now this car was a banger an old Ford but it could get me and my mates to the pub no bother and me with a pot leg as driver.

This became known to the authorities when a constable spotted my heap in the car park of a local pub. "And who owns that car with all the stickers on it ...apart from the one in the window that says it is taxed," he said to all present. "Err mm me" I volunteered. "Next time I see it", he said "I want to see a tax disc on it, alright!" Nodding affirmative we moved rather rapidly stage left and vacated the premises. The next day I was hauled in front of my O.C. and told in no uncertain terms that my car was off the road until it was taxed and insured.

That night we bowled off down town as usual.

The next day I was pulled in by the provost sergeant, "I have removed your distributor cap and your car stays impounded until it is taxed and insured." So, a pal and I went to a local scrap yard and we managed to get a distributor cap for a six-cylinder engine, mine being four, but what the hell, it'll work. And with lots of farting and starting we got the car mobile again for another foray down town.

There were several commonwealth soldiers billeted with us and a couple of them from West Africa we, got attached to. Hauling them in with us one night we invited them to join us on a foray into Bournemouth and in particular to The Boscombe Ballrooms. A Guaranteed pick-up with the local talent, No error.! How naïve can you get!

Having been away from the UK for several years and inter-mingling with all races it didn't percolate into my noggin that inviting our black brethren soldiers into a white society was just not on. From the moment of entry our comrades were snubbed and humiliated by the girls of Bournemouth. It was embarrassing for us to see our guests turned down again and again, …it was bad enough for us but we were used to it as squaddies. For them. I don't know.

We got out of there and went to a pub instead…at least that was a lot friendlier. Ashamed of my own I have to say. What is wrong with these people?

Where did it change? I'd heard of American Army consternation when English girls went out with black G.Is as a matter of course, when they were posted here in WW2, so what was the problem? Beats me.

I was presented with a Ghanian shirt by one of the lads and still have it to this day, a real gift, given in true friendship. Thanks, my old comrade. And years later I met an old veteran in Nigeria who could still recount his days with affection, of the time he won his medals in Burma with the Fourteenth Army, fighting the Japs.. He at least was sorry we had left these countries to the politicians and gangsters, crooks and chancers that followed Independence.

Our empire was still looked on in some quarters at least as a force for good…shame to the politicians here and there who loused it all up.

Following our foray to Bournemouth I was banged up in the OC's office once again.

"That's it." he yelled, "Get the hell off my camp, go away, in fact take two weeks leave…go away and stop annoying me!"

And as I left his office, he shouted, "….and for another thing, I've just received a signal from your unit, you've just been promoted to Lance Corporal.

so, congratulations …. but *fuck off* anyway!"

And so, I left Bovington….selling my car for seven shillings and sixpence before I left.

This car came back to haunt me a year later when I came back to England after Benghazi. A policeman had me called to the guardroom to enquire why I had abandoned it in a lay-by. Not me I said as I had sold it and was overseas when the offence had occurred. My name was the last registered owner in the log book but the constable accepted my plea and that was the last I heard of it.

My first car cost a tenner and it was a dog but we had some good times in it. Dodgy steering, farting engine, smoke coming through the floorboards…it rattled along, needed petrol occasionally and responded to the odd sing-a-long as we returned to camp…. you can't ask for more.

And no it was never taxed nor insured.

CHAPTER 7

RETURN TO LIBYA & FIRE

Back in Wavell Barracks and all was as before. I still enjoyed the desert exercises but now as a Lance Corporal I had progressed to having to take a responsible job.

When in camp I became the cinema projectionist for the camp theatre. I collected cinema posters and I wish my collection hadn't been trashed when later events occurred. Just think of the value of those posters today…. from the mid-sixties, Dr No, & other James Bond films, Cool Hand Luke, The Ipcress File. Ah! Well.

If I remember correctly, I also started smoking at this time, why this should be so I don't know. Rothmans King Size. I have several photographs of me with a ciggie hanging from my lips and a beer in hand.

Wavell Barracks from the air. Twynham tin huts for the most part as our barracks and some married quarters on the far left.

Part of my time was spent babysitting for the NCOs when they wanted a sitter. My troop Sergeant and my troop Corporal both relied on me to look after their youngsters and I was quite happy to do this, they paid and it was pleasant to be in a family environment.... until. One night after a power cut, I left candles burning in the kid's bedroom and soon the whole room was alight. Batting down the flames, as the children clapped and cheered, was the least of my worries as the next morning showed a dresser cabinet very distressed and burnt out. Needless to say, I wasn't asked to baby sit again by that family. Talking about babies.

Out on the town one night, on my one and only visit to the night clubs of Benghazi I tried to sell my mate Baby-Face, so called because of his chubby baby looks. Not all of my fault but we ended up in a taxi back to camp....and no fare, we'd spent it all on beer at the club. 'Face' had conked out next to me and I had to persuade the taxi-driver to take us the last 3 miles back to Wavell Barracks. "Ginghi-wallah," I said, pointing at Face. "He much, jig -a -jig." Thumbs up! "Take us to Wavell and you can screw my mate all night long I offered.

The taxi driver with a gleam in his eye as he eyed up Face and with a hard on cottoned on fast and drove us to the main gates of Wavell Barracks, salivating on his clutch, only to be frustrated at the last minute as I hauled a sleepy Face out of his cab and I dragged him to the safety of our perimeter fence.

The perimeter fence included the ammunition compound. And there happened one of the strangest events of my experience. A soldier was always posted there on guard duty and on this particular occasion the chap on guard deserted his post to play football on the adjacent pitch. He was spotted by the guard commander and was summarily hauled up on Squadron orders.

The usual case was read out and he was asked if he accepted the OC's punishment. He declined and had had to be sent in front of the Colonel, for a heavier sentence. Once again, he declined to accept any punishment, nothing else was left but a General Court Martial and an even bigger sentence was forthcoming. I remember him sitting in the barrack room reading a copy of Queen's Rules and Regulations and we all thought he was mad to continue his intransigent stance, but we admired his balls standing up for himself against a certain long-term gaol sentence. Comes the Court Martial and he dispensed with his defence counsel and answered for himself. *Phew!* Well. He had the answer.

He was charged with deserting his post, a very serious offence and the cunning blighter took them on. He proved that the guard commander had not read him his orders and so he did not know where his post was! Playing football whilst on duty was not the crime mentioned. His case was dismissed.

This chap left soon after that and the next we heard was that he had joined the Australian Army and was serving in Vietnam. Lo! And behold! He was then Court Martialled by the Australian Army.

The only bloke I knew to be court martialled by two armies! Apparently, he had come to an arrangement with an American unit to patrol a road meeting half-way to switch responsibilities for a convoy protection. This failed to happen and the Vietcong thumped the convoy. How he got out of that one I don't know and that's the last I heard of our erstwhile hero. But sometimes we got away with it as my next little escapade proved.

I mentioned the families bar earlier in down-town Benghazi, the Ace of Clubs, a NAAFI bar for families, complete with white women and easy chairs. We peons, the singlies had to make do with a slovenly beer bar and Formica tables and the usual detritus of a downstairs room set aside for the lower classes. Not happy at this I and my mate Bob Fields, of Hong Kong fame as the Matt Monroe episode showed, decided to invade the upstairs family lounge.

The bar-man used to family etiquette and refinement made the mistake of refusing us a drink and demanded that we leave. Whereupon we both yanked him over the bar and proceeded to serve ourselves amidst broken glasses and spilt bottles. No sooner had this altercation started then the military police arrived.

Bob was dragged out first and I raged at the injustice of it all when I too had my collar felt and I too joined him in the 'paddy wagon' .... driven to camp and dropped off at the guardroom for a night in the cells. I was charged the next day, believe it or not, with "Using foul language in the presence of females!"

As to the Ace of Clubs, well in the next chapter of events this locality was the reason for my near demise. The six-day war in 1967. The Israelis thumped the Egyptians no error in the first day, shooting up their air force and ground forces early on. Of course, the rest of the Arab world went into conniptions. How could this be without US and Western connivance as in 1956? So, it spilled over into Libya. The first targets in Benghazi were the American Embassy and the British Embassy, which we were tasked to defend. Rioters were soon on the scene. The Americans decamped to the British Embassy when their Embassy was attacked and our local British infantry battalion was soon throwing a cordon of bayonets around the British Embassy to protect all and sundry. Stalemate. The rioters went in search of easier targets. Meanwhile the rioters had set fire to nearly all of the petrol stations and were attacking any perceived western property.

Some of our armoured cars had been attacked when going into the town to escort families out and in the process my old driver Mac from my Tidworth days had been struck with a cobblestone in the head as a memento of that visit. (He later painted it black with the inscription, ' Presented to L/cpl McIntyre by the people of Benghazi.') I was in the command post at Wavell Barracks as a radio operator when the call came to relieve folk barricaded in the Ace of Clubs NAAFI and about to be assailed by rioters. A force was gathered to be led by our Sqn. Officer Commanding, a major. At this point my opposite number in the HQ, on the OC's crew who was to go with the relieving party asked to switch roles. Never volunteer my dad had always said, but with the chance of riding into action to the rescue, who could refuse? Well one chap did.

I gave him my seat in the command post and within minutes we were away, roaring off in the Saracen command vehicle, Twit!

A Saracen APC Command Vehicle. Similar to the one in which our SHQ Saracen was set on fire, me included! Six of us, shut in and cooking at 500c, the skin was flayed off us!

We drove to the British Embassy, one Saracen armoured car with a crew of four. The Sqn. OC, a driver and Ronnie and myself as radio operators. Following us was a 3-ton Bedford with 20 men kitted out for riot duty.

Well almost.

In this day and age, you would expect riot shields, CS grenade launchers, baton rounds, body armour and batons at the least, but no our chaps had dustbin lids and hockey sticks, for head protection they at least had their steel helmets! Moving through the infantry cordon we could see garages burning, petrol stations zooming up in flame and clouds of smoke, shops on fire and rubble from collapsed buildings. There must be something in all of us that loves destruction and violence. I know I felt the exhilaration of it all. It was exciting! At this point Ronnie and I made the decision to open up the only armament we carried. Notwithstanding the OC's orders *not* to open the box, as it had to be returned to the QM. Intact!

Shades of the QM at Islandwana in the Zulu wars who was partly to blame for the massacre of 1200 British and levy troops by refusing to open up his ammunition boxes. If he had and he had handed out the cartridges, the sustained fire of the British red-coats would have sickened the Zulus enough for them to pull out of their attack. As it was running out of bullets, they were overwhelmed by the Zulu Impis.

We began opening up the CS grenades. (Tear Gas). These came in tins, which had to be opened like a corned beef can with a 'key' and then wrapped in heavy duty plastic, we struggled to get a half a dozen opened before we entered the fray. The safety pins were the last bloody factor. Bloody great steel pins, bent over of course; and I would defy any Hollywood actor to come along and pull one of those pins with his teeth!

A trip to his million-dollar dentist would have followed, along with a new set of teeth! Ever tried to open a beer bottle with your teeth? Don't!

Along with that we tried to get the OC to get the 'battle hatch' for the driver shut. "No," he said. And that was our downfall. The wide-open hatch was OK for normal driving and it could be closed, restricting the drivers view but ultimately safer.

As we approached the area of the Ace of Clubs we stopped to pick-up two MPs in civvie clothes…. for their safety for crying out loud! The OC wanted directions to the Club, so he ordered these two to get into the APC. He could of course have simply asked me as I had recently been chucked out of there …. but it was his *Indaba*. Turning onto the main dual carriage-way leading to the club we were confronted by the main mob of rioters. There were at least a thousand of the buggers, all in a frenzy and not in the least put out by this pathetic force.

A few .30 bullets overhead or even into them might have changed their tune, but we weren't armed. More's the pity.

The squad of 20 men with their dustbin lids and hockey sticks de-bussed from the following lorry and were immediately overwhelmed by the mob before they could even form up. Ignominiously they were battered back and got the hell out of there as fast as they could.

Our Saracen then became the main target for the rioters. I was at the open back hatch throwing CS grenades into the mob as fast as Ronnie could get them to me. It was useless. I was hit several times with rocks in the upper body and my head was bleeding as my helmet had already been knocked off. I threw my last CS grenade and dropped back inside, closing the hatch as I went.

I was concussed from a rock and bloody from a head wound but a worse scene confronted me as I collapsed onto the floor.

The two MP's and Ronnie were still unharmed but our driver Jimmy was knocked out and under a pile of timber and rocks which had been rammed through the opened front hatch.

You can't say I didn't try to warn you to shut it, but would you listen? Nah!

The OC after being hit with rocks and almost unconscious was laid out under his turret, and mumbling, "Can anyone drive this thing?" He was mumbling because he had a broken jaw.

I stared at him in disbelief and he stared back in a queer kind of shocked curiosity. We were both in shock and amazed that this was happening.

We were immobile and trapped. And nobody moved to change anything. Worse was to follow.

Suddenly we were drenched in petrol as the rioters swarmed over our stalled vehicle. Where had the petrol come from you may well ask? Well, we went into a riot with jerry cans of petrol strapped to the sides of the vehicle, how clever is that? Anyway. Too late! Within seconds the whole bloody thing went up with a WHOOF!

I felt a dull concussion which made my ribs ache with a thud as the breath was sucked out of me in the flash. This can't be happening to me I thought…but it was. We cooked at about 500oC and the skin was flayed off us. I was at the back door as we screamed in agony, I booted the door open and fell out into the mob. I was in mortal agony and the kicks and blows from the mob hardly registered, I got on my feet, still on fire and I pushed my way through the rioters, falling into a doorway and beating out the flames. Lying there some of the crowd came to attack me and helped to extinguish the last of the flames by giving me another kicking. Fine chaps that they were.

In the words of the poet, *I was well and truly fucked!*

I never saw any of the others emerge and I never saw any one of them on the street, I was on my own surrounded by a raving mob but for the time being left alone. I don't even remember seeing the burning Saracen.

I suppose some of the rioters were burnt too and I just hope *Allah the compassionate* looked after them because I as sure as hell wouldn't have. As to the besieged staff at The Ace of Clubs whom we were meant to rescue, well they vacated the premises whilst we were getting our arses kicked, smart fellows!

Where to next? The British Embassy was closest and they had troops, so I set off. I was a mess.

My head was bloodied and my face burnt, with skin hanging off it, my arms had crispy skin hanging in strips and my legs were deeply burnt and large blisters were forming where the petrol had burnt the longest.

I had kicked off my desert boots as they had been on fire, so all I stood in was the remnants of my short sleeve shirt and my khaki trousers. Staggering back to the Embassy I came across a group of youths who had missed all of the fun at the main event and they immediately surrounded me. My only weapon was my web belt, complete with brass buckles and I removed this, wrapped it around my bloody hand and threatened them with it. I don't know to this day whether it was this or the sight of me that put them off. I didn't know that I had lost most of my hair, no eyebrows, no eyelashes, and my face burnt off, blackened and with a bloody nose and cut lips, bleeding profusely and with my scalp laid open. They decided to leave me to go on my way. I then staggered into the Army cordon around the Embassy and wasn't in the least upset by their horrified looks as I lurched to safety.

My troop Sgt, seeing me at the Embassy later said, "I didn't even recognise you; you were in such a mess."

The official Regimental history of that event had; *'A Lance Corporal ran to the British Embassy.' Ran?* I could hardly stagger never mind run, but that's historians for you, particularly the officer class who write this nonsense in between their polo club and horse-riding activities.

Much, much later I learned that my OC, had even forgotten that I was casevaced along with the others back to the UK for extensive surgery. He maintained in an interview in 2014 that as the first out of the Saracen I wasn't badly burned and that I had got back relatively unharmed, returned to duty and wasn't sent back to the UK with the others! This calumny from him exists in several museums and histories around the country as part of our Regimental verbal history; which I had helped to compile in 2014 by interviewing over 30 officers and men with their experiences from WW2 to the present day. So much for memory!

But then I can only put it down to the fact that as an officer he had a room all to himself whilst we five were all in the same ward; too many names to remember I suppose.

As one of the Military Police Corporals, Dave C., later said, "If you hadn't kicked that back door open when you did, we'd have all still been in there!"

I was nearest at the back I suppose but I also knew the door would stick and the only way to open it was to give it a bloody good kick.

Well, the OC was entitled to his view, after all he was the officer that put us there in the first place.

Surprisingly in 1992 at a Regimental reunion I learnt that he had been a Lieutenant in the 1950's when my dad had been a Sergeant. Indeed, I have a photograph of the two of them in 1950 marching out of Barker Barracks, Paderborn, West Germany.

He wasn't a bad Colonel when we served once again, he as Colonel and me as Recce Troop Leader. However, I didn't forget nor forgive the time that he had had allowed the drivers hatch to stay open and refusing to allow C grenades to be used.

I didn't agree with those that called him, 'Scarface,' due to his injuries, sustained that day, we did have a shared experience, that no one should have shared and he copped the worst. Anyone who thought different, hadn't been there.

So, there we were all six of us, stinking the place to the heavens, like mouldy cheese left to kick up a row in the cupboard. The others had escaped the inferno and had been escorted to a Libyan Military hospital, almost next door to the scene. We were all tucked up in bed in the British Military Hospital in Wavell Barracks with the nurses fighting to get at us, whilst the rest of the Regiment was 'bombed up', and facing off an Arab battalion surrounding the camp who wanted to restore some face to their defeat by the Israelis. I knew nothing of this as I was out for the count for four days. Calm prevailed but we had to wait another ten days until we could get permission to be flown out. Meanwhile in the heat the stink of our condition got worse. My troop Sgts. wife held her nose and did all that she could for me, bless her cotton socks! As did my 2i/c who wrote both to my parents and to my fiancée, as we remember was Maria in Ireland. If you have ever been burnt or cut yourself, as we all have at one time or another, a scab forms over the wound. Well, imagine our scabs. My whole face was a scab as were the exposed arms, from wearing short sleeves. My legs just had deep holes in them where the blisters had been, but the hands and arms needed constant movement to crack the scabs, and on a daily basis our physiotherapist made us move the joints until the blood ran.

When we smiled or grimaced, blood ran from our cracked faces.

No wonder the nurses sometimes decided that the monotony of the obstetrics ward or general medical ward was preferable.

Anyway, we had to get to a colder climate as the infection and resultant smell of suppurating bodies in the heat was bound to lead to nastier complaints. So, with an escort our ambulances took us to Benina airport and we were flown to Malta. We spent a night with the lovely ladies at the Navy hospital and were then given priority on an RAF jet to the UK. I regret to say that because we were stretcher cases, several disgruntled folks lost their flight to the UK. We took up the best part of 20 seats in our stretchers on a VC10. Arriving in the UK, the back door was opened and our stretchers were loaded onto fork lift trucks, trundled across the tarmac and off-loaded into Wessex helicopters to be flown directly to RAF Halton, burns unit.

Say what you like about Britain and the Armed Forces but you couldn't get better than that. What a smooth operation. Army, Navy, Air Force, melded into one. From Middle East to the UK. Superb organisation! I tip my hat off to those who organised our casevac. (Casualty evacuation).

The first night we were there in RAF Halton a TV was installed in our ward and we watched, 'The Likely Lads,' a TV sitcom of Geordie life, which most of us had never seen previously. We were in tears of laughter, the blood running down our faces as the scabs cracked and the night nurse had to turn it off to save us from further damage. I bet the TV cast never knew about that!

The next bit wasn't so funny. As we all needed skin grafts, we had to have saline baths every day to scrape away the scabs until the skin became clear enough to take a graft.

I was lucky, my skin started to heal quickly, others took longer.

Ronnie had a tattoo and this came away as he was being scraped. He kept this strip of skin in a phial of formaldehyde and he still has it to this day, on his mantelpiece, over fifty years later.

I can't praise the surgeons and the staff at RAF Halton enough. They were professional and dedicated to their work. God Bless them. One of our surgeons who did the skin grafts was The Queen's Surgeon. Dunno his name but he was bloody good at it. With small 'postage stamp' scraps of skin taken from healthy skin he stuck them back on us, bit by bit until they melded together forming a new surface. It was interesting watching our skin grow. I always say from then on, "I was arse about face!"

We were sent out from there and apart from the odd return for check-ups we began to recreate our lives once again, whole. There were pilots at RAF Halton from WW2 still trying to reconstruct their faces and Germans who had survived recent Starfighter crashes.

One chap losing his face when his oxygen mask was ripped from his head by a rescuer. His face still attached to the rubber seal.

My sister-in-law pronounced that I wasn't the same person after Benghazi and perhaps she was right. I was still engaged to Maria after two years overseas but that was all. The whole thing fell flat and we decided to end it. Many years later I still feel guilty at taking advantage of this innocent Irish lass but we were no longer in love so what was the use.

There was no marriage as promised. After she had gone, I bought a car instead with my savings from the wedding! What a cad! So, I entered late sixty-seven, still single and still as dim, almost kicked out of the British army due to my medical down-gradings.

My saviour was our Regimental second in Command, a man of foresight and intelligence.

"The Regiment will return from overseas very soon and I task you two corporals on the advance party with a job that should suit you both." Indicating myself and Taff Evans, "You are to set up a welcoming home coming for the Regiment, we will get a dance organised and your main job, is………..to get girls to attend!"

Now anybody who has ever been to an army dance knows that, women are always in short supply. Apart from NCO's and their wives, spare females are at a premium, ten blokes to one female were the usual ratio.

He couldn't have picked two better emissaries. Taff was blonde, handsome and I was a walking hero with a car. What a job! We had carte blanche to go wherever we wanted, and we did just that; on army petrol of course. OK, smart arse you tell me where you would have started in Weeton Camp a few miles out of Blackpool, which was where we were then posted to after Libya & Cyprus. Holiday makers were of no use as this dance was for three months hence.

We decided to keeping transport to a minimum and set up six bus runs to pick the ladies up from several strategic points across the Fylde Peninsular.

We visited all of the major stores and hospitals in Blackpool, Kirkham and Preston. Woollies, M&S, the colleges and the places where girls were to be found.

We were chatting up the shop girls and the nurses on their lunch-breaks and offering paradise.

Come on! A free bus timetable and a safe lift home, a sumptuous buffet, free drink, dance to the best of music and best of all, take your pick from hundreds of sex starved presentable young men; just returned from overseas. What girl could resist?

This was set for March 1968 when the Regiment was complete again, after almost three years of being on different overseas postings, Hong Kong, Aden, Libya & Cyprus.

Well, we didn't pack the buses but we got more than enough, and from that dance there were several long-term marriages, mine amongst them.

1969..........and just about then as we were posted to West Germany, the Northern Ireland troubles started ....but that's another story into the Seventies.

Printed in Great Britain
by Amazon